The Business of Personal Relationships

HOW TO USE EVERY TOOL AVAILABLE TO INCREASE PROFIT, PRODUCTIVITY, AND PEACE OF MIND

Jane Beaudry

Copyright © 2016 Jane Beaudry

All rights reserved. No part of this publication may be reproduced, distributed or transmitted in any form or by any means, including photocopying, recording, or other electronic or mechanical methods, without the prior written permission of the publisher, except in the case of brief quotations embodied in critical reviews and certain other noncommercial uses permitted by copyright law. For permission requests, write to the publisher, Develop Mastery Press, P.O. Box 52785, Atlanta, GA 30355, "Attention: Permissions Coordinator."

The Business of Personal Relationships/ Jane Beaudry —1st ed.

ISBN 978-1974692538

Contents

1. Where Do Our Choices and Truths Really Come From?............1
2. Not So Uncommon................5
3. What Is Your Reality?............13
4. Why Ask for Help?............19
5. Full Potential Highest Self............29
6. Is Something Holding You Back?............37
7. It's All About You, Relationship with Yourself.....47
8. Correcting Your Past, Giving Yourself Permission to Be the Catalyst............55
9. Coming to America............63
10. How You Treat Yourself Is How the World Treats You............65
11. Your Conscious Mind............69
12. Your Subconscious Mind............75
13. Putting the Conscious and Subconscious Together 85
14. You Can Get Results Faster!............95

This book is dedicated to those who appreciate what it takes to be a true leader and master executive excellence ... who are willing to help the world around them for the greater good of all.

Acknowledgments

I would like to acknowledge:

My parents, who taught me that "life is a learning process," as well as the values that I find in life and in the many business relationships I've experienced. My two older brothers, who taught me about survival and forgiveness.

My husband, Stephen, who expresses his own unique brilliance every day, and for his utter support of my desire to make a difference in my own way.

Friends, who have been kind, patient, and there for me when I needed support. You are often, at heart, my true family. You remind me that successful people ask for help when they need it!

The path and life I have chosen, and the individuals I have been privileged to serve. May the work we've done together continue to assist you in being of greater service to yourself, others in your life, and the world at large. You were also my teachers, inspiring me to continue to grow and evolve in ways that create results that work!

Every now and then, I discover a person who is a model of true leadership. With a grateful heart, I seek to mirror specific qualities of these individuals. I have many role models, and have adopted the parts of them that are best suited to my own path to success being in service of my clientele.

All the many teachers, coaches and trainers (business, academic, spiritual, life), authors, and persons of wisdom by way of the written, audio and oral word, conferences, research, research institutions, and looking beyond what is typically recognized toward the possibilities of the whole and infinite that life can take on.

And, of course, Ann McIndoo, Jim House, and Dr. Andreas Boettcher who assisted me in getting this book out of my head. Great appreciation also goes to the support I received from Cole Gustafson at Kevin Anderson & Associates, especially Erin McKnight for her understanding and quality editing, and my long-time assistant and support, Kristin Hankins

Foreword

We've all had bosses and have been under the influence of "leaders." Some, if you're lucky enough, made a positive difference in your life and in the organization that they were charged with leading. Others perhaps left scars on you and on their organization, holding both back from higher potential. Either way, healing can take place. Whether you are aware of it or not, your Full Potential Highest Self has always been within you and can be awakened. . . . . . even if you've never met your complete true self, even if what you're reading seems impossible right now.

What is your Full Potential Highest Self? Much like within each seed is the full, natural, and magnificent potential of a plant when tended to and allowed to flourish, within nature, science, quantum physics, psychology, behavior, and spirituality is the energy of life. You too came into this life with all the potential that when tended to you could become; it's innate, even if you've never experienced it. The reason it sounds foreign is because the society we were born into doesn't acknowledge its own Full Potential Highest Self, so how could it recognize it in you when you were born? It's no one's fault. At the same time, it's still available and you can have access to it.

I have been asked for years to write this book. Many people wanted me to tell their story of transformation from the work we did together. When you're busy helping people, it's tough to find the time to write such a book. In fact, I started writing a similar book around five years ago. But this particular book has come about because I realized there is a specific group of people who I wanted to influence the most . . . the leaders, the doers, the achievers, and the influencers on this planet. These are often businesspeople at the top of their field, or perhaps political influencers, or entertainers, who wanted to achieve more and also improve the world beyond themselves.

Leaders come in many forms and often feel isolated, as they are looked upon as supposedly being or having to be perfect. It's true that they are often the smartest person in the room. At the same time, they too are human with not only a brilliant mind, but also patterns that are sometimes unhelpful, making them less effective than they could otherwise be.

Perfectionism is a double-sided sword. One side pushes one to grow and become more accomplished and successful, often setting an example of what might be possible for others. The other side of perfectionism is frequently an experience of worry, overwhelming anxiety or massive stress, a suffering through of life wherein there's no such thing as satisfaction or self-acceptance, even with "success" for themselves and others.

How many perfect people have you met? (Seriously!) I suspect none. Not even you, if you'll let your guard down long enough to tell yourself the truth.

So how can it be that accomplished college presidents, C-suite leaders, entertainers, political figures, religious leaders, and the like feel "less than"? Or that they are not good enough and then find themselves turning to a life of perfectionism that ultimately causes anxiety, criticism, sometimes depression, unhealthy choices, and more?

Introduction

I wrote *The Business of Personal Relationships* because we've been lied to by the misunderstandings and misperceptions from history and from our early childhood with unhelpful messages from ourselves and our environment that turn into unconscious limiting and controlling beliefs. We lie to ourselves about ourselves, to those around us, and about what's possible. The lies become filters through which we limit ourselves and our world. This ultimately causes problems with our feelings, reactions, relationships, and the bottom line. The first problem is that you don't even realize that you are lying to yourself or that others are lying to themselves or you. I'm not saying this is intentional or conscious. We all know it's easy to be misunderstood or surprised to discover that we have misunderstood others (although you may hate to, or rarely, admit it).

It's a common trait for humans to assume that we are right; leaders are no exception. You may not have learned that when we unknowingly don't have accurate or complete information, our minds want to automatically fill in the blanks with data that is not always helpful, much less accurate. It's call projection.

Perhaps you've heard the more recent research that most people make up their mind about us within the first three seconds. It's easy to judge and be misjudged. How can someone possibly know you, or you know them, in three seconds? Many people live a lifetime and don't even know themselves as much as they assume they do. How can we when 90% of our brain is the unconscious or subconscious?

Does this describe you or someone you know? Do you find yourself feeling frustrated with your profession or in your personal life? Do you struggle with emotions that cause conflict in yourself or others? Do you want to blame the world around you when others don't agree with you or see life the way you do? Are you a perfectionist? Controlling? Angry? Isolated in a sea of people?

This book will help you to understand yourself and those around you in a less speculative way and will make understanding and listening easier, no matter the relationship.

Jane Beaudry
2016

CHAPTER ONE

Where Do Our Choices and Truths Really Come From?

In the Western world, at least, we've been told that we all have choice. However, it is rare that any one of us actually exhibits authentic true choice.

You may want to argue with me right now, but please take a moment to consider the following: What seems like choice is really a reflection of your prior environmental exposure, coupled with your unique and limited perception and interpretations of life.

A straightforward example of your perceived choice is the fact that each person sees life in a way that is uniquely theirs and theirs alone and that is often referred to as "common sense." What seems like common sense to you is different to everyone else. Consequently, most people mistakenly believe that their perception is **the truth**. So who's right?

The Business of Personal Relationships

As we talk about facts or truth, we are more frequently influenced by our unconscious programs and patterns that are, in reality, a compilation of the unique meaning we give or get from our environment and our experiences. These influences are imbedded into our belief system by the age of ten and beginning as early as the third month in our mother's womb.

The chapters in this book offer examples of how very smart people, like you, and who are often thought of as being at the top of their game, got unstuck from their unconscious blocks and were able to move to a state of freedom by discovering *How to Utilize Every Tool Available to Increase Profit, Productivity, and Peace of Mind by Uncovering Your Full Potential Highest Self.*

The names of my clients shared herein have been changed to protect their privacy.

Each chapter includes facts and stories that you can perhaps relate to. And just maybe you have some secrets or unresolved issues that your position at the top makes it hard for you to talk about. And then there's the challenge of how to get those unresolved issues resolved.

Let me assure you that you are not stuck with no place to turn. You can become free of those patterns that do not serve you and maybe never did. The benefits will be priceless and you can become free! You can become the connected leader because you will be able to safely connect with yourself and release whatever is holding you back, whether you're aware of it or not. You know that "feeling," don't you? After all, even you are human! Wouldn't it be nice to feel good being human?

Ultimately, wouldn't it be transformative to discover a powerful and balanced being inside yourself that could support you in expressing your Full Potential Highest Self for the rest of your life? You can!

CHAPTER TWO

Not So Uncommon

To the outside world, my client Morgan was considered a successful CEO. Who wouldn't be satisfied and happy with such an achievement? Morgan became successful on many levels—in business and socially—eventually achieving levels never dreamed of as a young person, maturing into senior management, then eventually becoming the esteemed CEO of a large national corporation. Yet in Morgan's heart of hearts, doubts and reservations sometimes emerged. Some of you may have doubts that hold you back from being your best self, or from feeling satisfied or peaceful in your inner and outer worlds.

This story is not so uncommon.

Like you, our leader is intricate, complicated and, although it was at first denied, in some ways a perfectionist. There was also something missing inside Morgan. You see, this CEO, like most, was a master at wearing the "game face," under even the most stressful of circumstances.

It's lonely at the top. Everyone says that, but only those at the top know how painful it can actually be. And no one gets to the top alone. *The Business of Personal Relationships* was written to talk specifically about what is not talked about in successful business relationships: YOU, the INNER YOU!

This Story May Not Be So Uncommon, But Is Rarely Spoken Of

During a heart-to-heart talk, Morgan revealed the experience of having panic attacks. This all seemed very strange and scary because Morgan was very smart and thought it would just pass. Oh, Morgan was extremely skilled and thought of as an effective leader, but with the pressures of the company, the investors, an enduring reputation, a stressful home life, and feeling overwhelmed, something had to change. Morgan was the leader of some 56,000 employees. And the goal was to expand internationally. Morgan hadn't felt so overwhelmed and out of control for many years.

Ultimately, Morgan came to recognize that the rut was getting deeper and that there was nowhere to turn and no one to talk to or be vulnerable with. All the while, this leader kept the "game face" on. But this was getting harder and more difficult to pull off.

Morgan was also confused and angry because having been so accomplished for some years, there was a time when nothing seemed out of reach by way of pure will, study, having the right support people, and hard work!

So what is the solution? Coaching? *Wrong!*

Turns out that executive coaching alone is not the answer, AND IT'S NOT JUST ME SAYING SO . . . In a *Harvard Business Review* article titled "The Very Real Dangers of Executive Coaches," the point was made that most coaches, at every level, *do not have the understanding or expertise to help people permanently evolve past* their internal struggles. Many coaches are not aware that *clients may refuse to do the work or even accept change, just for a start.*

That's why I developed my proprietary method I call The Beaudry Process that to this day produces a 95% client success rate.

So what happened that set Morgan free? We worked in person and by Skype when getting together wasn't possible. My goal with Morgan, as with every client, is to have him or her evolve with each meeting.

We began the first process with my customized interview. During this phase of our work, the CEO came to have new insights that led us to the second step.

You might find it interesting to know that more than 99% of what you know you learned unconsciously. Therefore, environment is key! I have not met anyone who grew up in a perfect environment. You may be the exception, but 99% or more of those around you are not the exception, and perhaps you aren't either.

During the next part of the process, we began using what I call Mindfulness. Part of this includes customized guided meditation that helped Morgan learn to relax. Turns out that Morgan had no idea what really being relaxed and calm inside was like. It felt foreign at first, but good. This alone helped my client be more mentally and emotionally in control. You've probably heard about emotional and social intelligence. This step was the beginning of accessing powerful resources within Morgan.

The next part of the process included the critical training component: whole-brain learning. Since we all come into this world without an instruction booklet, we spent time teaching Morgan how the mind works and how the mind affects the body, plus how we create and change habits and patterns.

This information proved to be such an empowering part of the process that our leader gained the skills to practice correcting negative self-talk on the spot on a daily basis. With my help as strategic advisor and emotional mentor, this insight created awareness and helped build Morgan's mental and emotional skills muscle.

Learning about whole-brain learning and the added behavioral component helped lead Morgan to self-understanding as well as a much-improved understanding of others.

Awareness or being more conscious of our thoughts is key! Can we successfully learn without becoming aware of what might be a better option? Can we possibly have choice without awareness? I think not!

The next steps included starting to strategically access and release old unhelpful patterns to make room for new positive possibilities and opening up to become a more powerful, creative, innovative, and effective leader.

I frequently made recordings during the processes so that they could be reinforced at home or in the privacy of Morgan's office. Morgan had homework, too, to speed up the rewiring of these new mind/body goals.

It's impossible to be completely self-objective. That's why having a strategic advisor to give you feedback is also required.

Following these steps included a combination of getting down to the root causes of the unhelpful habits, patterns, and blocks so they could be strategically corrected. Just because you know why you are the way you are doesn't always make you change, does it?

This part of the process allowed the client to make new mature choices to create new messages and beliefs that worked more effectively instead of continuing to replay the same old unconscious, unhelpful internal tapes. As a result, this leader was able to release those unhelpful inner patterns and fears at every level.

How we are when we're young tends to become more prominent as we get older, unless we do something about it. But rarely does anyone do anything about it! Because they don't know it's possible, most people end up arguing for their limitations or suffering in silence sometime for a lifetime. With behavioral and brain research on the rise for the last forty years, we've learned a lot about how we can influence the rewiring of our mind, thereby improving our responses to life and therefore our behavior.

I want to call out the myth that you're supposed to rely only on yourself. This is a myth because it's virtually impossible to be truly objective about ourselves. Successful people ask for help when they need it! And, without that objectivity and helpful feedback, you are holding yourself back from your greater good and full potential.

I love working with my leaders because you are motivated to grow to achieve greater success, yield inner peace and happiness, plus increase the bottom line through improved relationships in business and at home.

Morgan had lots of "aha" moments and experienced greater evolution with each meeting to get closer to awakening the full potential already inside. Those at work noticed changes for the better even if at first they had no idea what was making the difference.

Morgan's ability to lead a powerfully effective team improved tremendously as the evolution continued. The corporate bottom line increased by 30% that first year and is still moving in a positive direction at an impressive rate.

Productivity companywide has obviously increased, along with more positive attitudes and an updated company culture.

Of course, if individuals within the organization do not respond, Morgan sends them to me for evaluation and help. Through this process, the entire organization has also been able to determine a better fit for the employees' particular strengths or when necessary cut its losses when someone is found to be unwilling to align themselves with company values.

Morgan is excited again and proactive! As a leader, Morgan improved substantially, as did the whole company, especially when Morgan's Full Potential Higher Self showed up. Ah!

Company feedback revealed Morgan as being more approachable, open-minded, and no longer judgmental. The board of directors got reconnected and I worked with the team to enhance their leadership skills and goals. Everyone benefitted.

How often do you check in to see how your leadership is being received by those around you? No one grows without honest feedback.

And there was an added bonus that I wasn't aware of until much later! Morgan's spouse transformed! My client discovered that somehow during the growth process, the wonderful, adventurous person Morgan had been attracted to in the first place so many years before reemerged. And my client's relationship with their children . . . well, it took them a while to learn to trust a new respectful parenting style, but the family is now healing and drawing closer.

CHAPTER THREE

What Is Your Reality?

• Reality: Brilliant people sometimes forget they need others and the perspective of others.

• Reality: Leaders often have no one to talk to about their inner issues or conflicts.

• Reality: In order to create relationships that generate success for leaders, organizations, and countries, emotional and social intelligence is required.

• Reality: Emotional and social intelligence does not just happen.

• Reality: True objectivity is rarely present.

• Reality: Most leaders make the inaccurate assumption that they are in control of themselves, those around them, and their enterprises.

- Reality: Being trustworthy with self and others builds trust and openness.

If you are like some of my C-suite, business, and influence clients, you might believe that you are usually the smartest or most gifted person in the room. While this belief feels good and may be a quiet source of pride, there is also a downside in that it prevents you from accurately seeing and effectively using the resources you have at your fingertips: the world around you, all the human beings that work with and for you, or the outsiders with whom you could work interdependently. It, after all, is a common mistake to limit yourself to the notion that we only have two choices: independence and dependence. The third choice, interdependence, is often the fastest and most fulfilling way to increase success and achieve peace of mind.

If someone were to ask you, "Who's in charge of you?" it is almost certain that you want to say it is you—yourself. Yet we are so unconscious and can be so reactive that in any given moment we are really just repeating what we believe or assume rather than thinking truly objectively about what is before us or what might be a greater possibility for all or your dreams. This is also true of our memories of the past. Because of the limitations of our conscious mind, it is easy to misread our environment and make up our own version of reality. Unfortunately, this constraint also makes it easy to miss possibilities that could be in store for us, for others, and for your organization.

What does all this have to do with reaching the top of your game? People are complicated and intricate, and you're no exception. Life is competitive! Call it survival of the fittest—call it what you will. If you are a leader or an influencer, it is certain that at some point you have felt insecure or have experienced a "blockage" regarding some aspect of your life.

There are many words in the English language that individuals use to describe this deep discomfort, such as
- Frustration
- Anxiety
- Worry
- Depression
- Sadness
- Anger
- Dissatisfaction
- Teeth grinding
- Stress
- Conflicts or inappropriate emotional outbursts
- Aloneness or loneliness
- Insecurity all the way to panic
- Shame
- Feeling overwhelmed or experiencing inner emotional isolation
- Feeling regrets
- Going numb

- Self-critical
- Feeling helplessness
- Stuck
- Unhappy

It also shows up as fears related to:
- A deficit of some kind
- Bottom-line issues
- Anticipatory anxiety
- Public speaking
- Claustrophobia
- Flying
- Not being good enough
- Making a mistake
- A lack of confidence
. No exit plan
. Anxiety toward the future and the unknown

And, of course, leaders can be seen as critical and impatient and as possessing ineffective coping skills—leaving a wake of judgment, a lack of empowerment, and less-than-effective staff, when other measures would be more effective in building relationships, team cohesion, and increasing your bottom line. Sometimes leaders can even be seen as too soft or not strong enough to lead.

Leaders are often secretly worried and anxious about their legacy. When the time comes, many leaders will not have an effective exit strategy that leaves everything and everyone in their organization in great shape.

Bottom line, it is the fear of a lack of control or other unconscious limiting perspectives that scares many the most. Some would call it the fear of the unknown. Many people get caught up in the unknown world of what-ifs, and this usually creates a scary, negative, or depressive outcome, first in their mind, in their limited perceptions, and then through the choices they make.

All these ways of saying "I'm scared," whether internally or externally, to a large degree are creating self-sabotage, and also often self-criticism, "frustration," or anger.

When most clients come into my office, they know they don't feel right inside, but they don't always know what to call it and, more frighteningly, they don't know how to get rid of the heavy feeling that keeps them from moving forward into joy, freedom, fun, amazing success, happiness, and inner peace.

What do you worry about at 3:00 a.m.?

Most executives, corporate and political, professionals, and entertainers are scared to death to talk about their inner challenges and to ask for help. Since you're reading this, you may have already tried attending seminars, receiving coaching, and even seeing therapists. And maybe you blame the world around you, deny that your problems exist, described as "shoving it under the rug," or suffer in quiet desperation and under enormous pressure.

You may want to ask for help and you may even want the right person to know you could really use some help. You fear someone will use your vulnerability against you. You feel you can't trust anyone!

Yet you're fed up. You so desperately want to be done with the pain, agony, fears, and frustrations.

Where do you go to get the results you've always wanted? *The Business of Personal Relationships* was written to give you hope and to offer unparalleled options that may be just what you've been seeking. If you took a few minutes to consider what your ultimate life would be—if you could create and have whatever you wanted—what would your ultimate path and outcome look like?

CHAPTER FOUR

Why Ask for Help?

Why might you want to hear about *your* unconscious patterns and programs? Because everyone struggles from time to time, in different ways.

Many years ago, while I lived on Maui, I began working with top national and international leaders in business, academics, politics, and entertainment. They had come to realize that running to places like Hawaii wouldn't fix their internal struggles.

These top influencers and performers often secretly struggled with blind spots or unconscious blocks, while they wanted to be at their peak performance and feel at peace inside. They had tried coaching, therapy, medications, alcohol, or other ways to try to feel better. Ultimately, they wanted to feel strong and centered as well. However, these methods didn't offer the permanent pathway to peak performance and inner peace that they'd hoped for.

By the time I would meet them, these leaders and stars had come to realize either from their own awareness or because others had pointed it out that they were stuck in a rut or a recurring pattern. As smart, talented, resourceful, and intelligent as they were, it certainly didn't make their internal discomfort go away or their relationships improve.

And, sometimes coming from another culture or a different company or outlook, they struggled with culture shock and the inability to integrate so they could be at the top of their leadership game. Maybe they blamed others or even themselves. Either way, parts of their work and life were a struggle.

My clients had unconscious blocks that caused them to feel stressed, angry, anxious, overwhelmed, or insecure; they found themselves frequently taking out their frustrations on their staff, board, associates, cohorts, family members, and loved ones. Often, because these were blind spots, they couldn't comprehend the challenges and discomfort their behaviors were inflicting on those around them.

Most importantly, these clients were not operating professionally or personally at their peak potential. Some would know where their negative influences came from, but awareness still didn't fix the problem or pattern.

And they had NO ONE to confide in or to receive strategic advice from!

These clients wanted someone they could trust, someone they could open up to and feel safe with, someone who would confidentially and effectively help them grow beyond their unconscious issues. The Beaudry Process is a customizable process that works to resolve the unconscious blocks that hold you back from moving to your next level of mastery. With participation in and support of the process, my clients are able to reach a level of unsurpassed clarity. Follow-up is an integral part that ensures the permanence of the higher functioning level, effectiveness, and inner peace.

Finding Someone Who Cares and Who Knows How to Help You and Who You Can Trust

My own life has not always been filled with inner peace and freedom. I know all too well the painful feelings that my clients experience. I know the pain of being too afraid to ask for help. I know what being a perfectionist is all about. I was, in fact, raised by one. That's the good news and the bad news, isn't it? In retrospect, I came to understand how unaware I really was. As it is often said, "Hindsight is 20-20." I've been there and I'm sure you have too!

Like the top influencers and rainmakers, I work with today, I secretly struggled early on with my own blind spots—unconscious blocks—while simultaneously experiencing what I thought was my peak performance.

This journey of mine was not fast or easy. Yet over time, I evolved and experienced more than I could have ever hoped to achieve. As a result of getting the help I needed to secure my own deep inner development, my perspective on life was forever changed for the better. I began to feel internally stronger, healthier, and much happier.

I also discovered my calling. I knew that there were many leaders and top performers who were struggling with similar inner challenges that I was finally free from. I committed my life to helping these individuals. I have spent years studying, practicing, and researching developmental psychology, behavioral therapy, science, human anatomy and physiology, quantum physics, spirituality, and metaphysics, in addition to developing a flexible proven process that is customizable for each of my clients that I've come to call The Beaudry Process.

My deep understanding has come from a compilation of my own experience, education, training and certifications in business, executive, life, and health coaching, as well as in assessments and mindfulness plus guided imagery, to name a few, for the deeper and more permanent transformation.

In addition to mastering the techniques that provided the results I longed for, I also created powerful new distinctions and techniques that I refined while helping hundreds of successful leaders. Clients from around the globe now seek me out to discover their own Full Potential Highest Self.

You may be wondering if you, too, might experience these results that seem almost magical. While to my clients it may indeed seem like magic, it's actually backed by scientific evidence. Here's a taste of what my clients are saying:

You Can Too!

"To think that I was not operating at my full potential was counterintuitive to me at first. However, Jane helped me realize that I had achieved only a small fraction of what my full potential was. It has truly been transformative for me. Thank you, Jane!"—A.J.

"I didn't have anyone to confide in. I had read every book that I could find on having a positive mental attitude and overcoming fears. Quite frankly they seemed to have no effect. A thousand times more powerful than the best self-help book ever written is the value of The Beaudry Process. Once Jane understands who you are, she applies solutions custom-tailored to help you overcome obstacles, find inner peace and happiness, and achieve greater success. My business is now skyrocketing!"—Reed S.

"It was the most important meeting of my life. I was going before the entire state legislature to present the case for our agency funding. I never thought I could do it, but I was a huge success and got my points across! Working with you, Jane, did more for me than help me to overcome my fear of public speaking. My confidence has increased in all respects."—N. M.

"I had finally reached my goal of being hired as president of a major university when I just couldn't stand the pressure of feeling the massive panic every time I had to speak before a crowd of people . . . After all, I was asking them most often for money. I am happily relieved to say that I got past all that. Now I feel confident and more competent to get the job I was hired to do done! Thank you, Jane; I couldn't have done it without you . . . painlessly, too. You not only saved my career, health, happiness, and my legacy, but my overall life improved, including my relationships at home."—M.K.

This Book Will Change What You Think Might Be Possible for You and for Your Future

In the following chapters, you will discover overviews of case studies that will help you understand what is possible for you. Perhaps you want to change for the better, and for good—even finding more joy in life. You can have that, too!

Are you completely satisfied with your answers to the following questions?

- What is the quality of your own internal relationship?
- What is the quality of your relationships with others?
- What would others say about you?
- Are you really the leader, the spouse, the partner, the parent you need to be?
- Are you still blaming others, feeling guilt, or are you unforgiving of others or yourself?

Let's help you get these questions answered so you may open yourself to the possibility of discovering your Full Potential Highest Self and access and create the emotional, social, physical, financial, and cultural life you've always wanted and deserve.

Do you want a permanent transformation in those few areas that need it and that require special attention in a short time frame? Do you want to just get better as a leader?

As my other clients have discovered, you are way more than you think you are. Inner peace is possible when wholeness is not only in your grasp, but ready for you to take hold of.

Your greater capabilities will be revealed and are far more impressive than you ever imagined. Permanent change is possible. However, no one makes it there alone . . . really. It's good to finally tell the truth! Perhaps you've been living under the old belief that you have to go it alone, especially when it comes to your deep inner struggles, hurts, patterns, or fears.

Whether you are struggling on a daily basis with your board of directors, employees, clients and customers, your partner or spouse, or other family members, you can get the private and confidential care that you need—and your world will improve. You can become a better version of yourself. And this won't typically happen in the next coaching session or business training that you attend.

With The Beaudry Process, you will learn that only 10% of your physical brain is your conscious mind. All your emotions and unconscious responses are in the other 90% of your mind, your subconscious. If you want to change your deep inner feelings and unconscious reactions, you must tap into whole-brain learning, including the subconscious. At the same time, it's critical to learn to use your conscious mind more effectively. This combination is the fastest and most permanent way to help your brain get rewired to function at the level you deserve to operate at that can truly create more inner peace and effectiveness for you and those around you.

In *The Business of Personal Relationships*, you will learn interesting and thought-provoking information about your mind, how it works, how we are all influenced, and how you can quickly evolve.

You will learn that you can change faster working with my Method. Let's help you get your questions answered and discover how to get your issues resolved so you can open yourself to the possibility of discovering your Full Potential Highest Self and access and create the emotional, social, physical, financial, and cultural life you've always wanted.

You already know that unless you decide to change, you won't. You will learn that you can change faster working with the right person for you who is focused on helping you clear out old patterns and habits that do not serve you while at the same time helping you instill your greater self. You will learn that when you change, somehow the world around you will transform. People will want to be in service of you instead of feeling afraid of you. You can even learn to stop scaring yourself, as happens in some cases.

You will learn that successful people ask for help when they need it. This may frighten you at first because you may feel that you will be perceived as weak. It's true that few should ever know your deep inner struggles. It's also true that those around you experience the ramifications of your deep inner struggles because your reactions sometimes manifest in inappropriate and enduring ways.

This can change! You can evolve into the leader and influencer who finds joy and creates a culture that works for you and for those who are interdependent with you! Perhaps as you delve into this book you will hear your own voice or the unconscious voice of those who are close to you from time to time as you hear what others have experienced in this book during their transformation. There is a way. You can get the care and evolution you need.

In the end, you are unlimited potential and you can and will meet your Full Potential Highest Self, full of strength, brilliance, happiness, resourcefulness, and inner peace!

CHAPTER FIVE

Full Potential Highest Self

Wouldn't you like to awaken your own unique Full Potential Highest Self? Do you ever ask yourself, "What's really possible for me?" Do you limit yourself without even knowing it? We all do! No one is immune to being vulnerable and 99.9999% of us never have a consistent experience of who we really are or can become. Wouldn't it be wonderful if you could experience strength in a way that though you're vulnerable, you are not afraid and are instead more resourceful than you've ever been?

Have you ever imagined a you that you wish you could be? Powerful, yet at peace. Happy being productive. Joyful and creative.

Let me tell you about one of the many leaders who have come to me wondering if there was more.

What Happens When You Have It All?

The Business of Personal Relationships

At first, Mark didn't think he needed help. He was such a high achiever and certain that he'd reached the pinnacle in his career. He was sure he knew what inner peace was because he could access and had learned to enjoy inner peace during his daily thirty-minute meditation times. Mark was also a giver. He had helped many people up the corporate ladder and I could see this generosity in his attitude. He had worked hard to become increasingly humble. He felt successful and thought his life was fabulous!

During our interview, Mark was open and candid about his interesting history, including having come to the United States from abroad to attend college; his various personal and business relationships and becoming a father; his ascent into the corporate world; the mistakes that haunted him; the lessons he'd learned. At the end of our interview, he discovered that there might be more to him than he had ever imagined.

I don't usually meet people the way I met Mark, but his wife, also a professional, had come to see me and had benefitted from our visits. Mark, being the curious type, had asked if she'd mind that he came in to see me on his own. She was supportive and thrilled.

It was clear that Mark had excellent values and lived them, but he admitted that he hadn't always. As he opened up to me, he shared that he had worked hard to become the man he was at that point. However, he wasn't proud of some of his history.

As we talked, he also revealed his greatest fears:
1. That his deviant side would again gain power, as it had in the past. It had caused him to backslide in his relationships, leading to him being divorced with three children and having a failed business thanks to his drinking, gambling, and fooling around on his now ex-wife.
2. He might not be able to think things through.
3. He would struggle to maintain his higher standards and his spiritual side, keep no secrets from his new wife, and remain transparent.

Although I considered him younger than middle-aged, I was astounded to hear of the heights he had accomplished in his career. I could see he was highly educated, well-mentored, experienced, hardworking, and absolutely committed to evolving himself and reaching the top.

Yet as he sat in my office in the La-Z-Boy chair, he openly pondered if he could be even more successful. Well, who can't? I asked him first what success meant to him. So, of course, as we began to talk about what it meant for him, he shared with me his amazing relationship with his current wife and how he was happy and extremely valuable to his organization, as he'd previously been in numerous others. Some business peers were envious of his wisdom and position.

The Business of Personal Relationships

I've seen it plenty of times. Mark lived the dream, but didn't find true satisfaction as top dog. For a long while, being at the top of his profession was all he had lived for. Eventually, he found that all the power, money, and prestige in the world wasn't worth the stress and the pain of losses, such as the divorce from his first wife and being tugged at from the shareholders all the way down. Being the front man of the few organizations fortunate to have him as leader, he was highly respected and in many ways, a true winner for both himself and these companies.

Yet the price, for him, turned out to be too great. As we looked back on his life, he discovered that he'd emotionally abandoned himself and those loved ones he'd had made lifetime commitments to—his family members—for the business world. He eventually came to realize that he had also abandoned himself by living an unhealthy lifestyle. He was living the idea of work hard and play hard. However, he came to experience the often negative consequences that come along with that lifestyle. As Einstein said, "Too much is too much."

Everyone saw Mark as a massive success and he was willing to do whatever it took to succeed. Sometimes, when looking back, he wasn't always proud of what he had done. Mark eventually came to realize that he was not living as his authentic self. As he matured, he could see that his own integrity had become warped. There was pain.

At heart, Mark was a seeker. This quality, of course, is one of the valuable qualities that all top leaders possess. In Mark's case, however, he had shifted his focus from reaching the top of the corporate ladder to reaching to become a better man and a better human being: someone he could admire and who would lead those individuals who encountered him, even if only for a moment, simply by being in his presence.

After struggling for several years with the old disappointments and losses, he began to wake up and decided to seek a different path. He delved into developing himself spiritually and worked on evolving himself into being a healthy life partner, and subsequently found his current wife.

Mark worked harder than ever to become an increasingly conscious and aware human being. He looked for balance in his personal and home life. He thought he had to step down from being top dog to a role of vice president in which he could share his leadership and brilliance but not have as much pressure.

As we strategized, we reflected on what Joseph T. Hallinan, former writer for the *Wall Street Journal* and author of *Kidding Ourselves and Why We Make Mistakes*, asserts, "How we look without seeing, forget things in seconds, and are all pretty sure we are way above average," and Mark began to notice that he might have some biases, like most people, in the way he perceived himself and the world in general, especially as we began to explore what else might be possible for him.

I supported him—through the interview process, then tapping into his greater mind—to ultimately access his Full Potential Highest Self. You see, I believe we all come into this world with special gifts and talents. Because our parents, culture, and environment don't recognize that we even have a Full Potential Highest Self, each of us is virtually guaranteed to be suppressed in terms of what is possible for us.

It isn't every day that I meet someone as advanced as Mark, but I had a feeling that even he hadn't met his own Full Potential Highest Self . . . the part of him that is whole, yet available under the right circumstances even though it had been suppressed long ago. As a result of our time together, Mark discovered that it wasn't something he had to create but something that was innate.

Ultimately, he found inner peace and no longer had to hope that God would be his redeeming resource. He also felt more spiritually connected than ever. Once he integrated his Full Potential Highest Self, he felt secure within and his fear in turn subsided. He experienced the strength and inner peace he'd sought and discovered that he could trust himself.

He found a goodness in himself that was unshakable. He also found another fifty or so great qualities that were at various levels of development: still dormant, somewhat matured, or already on the scale of his ultimate development. These were now all available to him, fully matured, awakening more and more daily within himself as he worked on calling them forth to permanently reinforce these amazing qualities. He was delighted at this new and unique level of mastery—the man he had hoped he could be some day. This was home for him and enabled him to be even more effective, yet also more his own person. And, for the first time in his life, he felt relaxed and at home inside himself, even more empowered and secure!

The Full Potential Highest Self of every client is innate and accessible—as is yours

But first we have to do some "housekeeping" to rid ourselves of patterns that will prevent us from accessing this greater self within us, and once our Full Potential Highest Self becomes clear and we can make ourselves available to be integrated into our reality on a permanent basis.

CHAPTER SIX

Is Something Holding You Back?

At the beginning of the next break at the business seminar I was attending, I got a tap on my shoulder from a man named Bob who was sitting directly behind me. You see, several times over the course of the training, the trainer had made positive remarks about the strategic advisory support I provided, including about the Method's potential value that I could bring to the leaders who made up the audience. The trainer also made a point of commenting on the strict confidentiality of my work with clients.

Bob and I spoke briefly during that short break, as he had already decided to seek me out. He asked for my card and told me he would call me. He felt hopeful that he could get the help he needed and was curious about the Full Potential Highest Self. We shook hands. His palms were sweaty. My heart went out to him.

Although we live on different sides of the country, Bob made an appointment with me and we soon began our work together. He confided in me that he had tried everything and, by this time, he felt helpless and hopeless at controlling his inner critic—the internal voice that criticized and second-guessed everything he did. At first when we would talk via Skype, it was obvious he would sweat.

Your Unconscious Mind Is Holding You Back

During our first meeting, Bob also confided in me that he had been limping along for what felt like his entire lifetime, and he didn't know why.

Bob, a business owner, felt he had a lot to contribute to his clients, potential clients, and his community. However, he was confused, in a state of near inner panic, and fearful. He didn't know why! At first he thought if he just knew why, everything would be fine and he could flourish with confidence and inner peace.

"Just knowing why" is often the "booby prize" when it doesn't make you or your life change; this is largely the problem with using coaching alone to work through inner and outer challenges—even traditional therapy typically takes a long time for transformation to occur. The methods I offer, on the other hand, are totally results-oriented and can be permanent! We work together as quickly as possible, but follow up periodically to check in and reinforce anything necessary to create permanent transformation. Sessions are sometimes three to five hours long, geared for evolution at each meeting, but typically taper down to one-hour follow-ups.

Bob had a lot to learn about himself and about what was possible for him. He knew he was smart, yet his self-talk was negative much of the time, even though he had tried hard to be positive. Whether he was at the office supposedly working—mostly worrying, feeling anxious, and procrastinating—or at home with his family, he felt that he wasn't good enough. He was afraid of many things, including that he wouldn't make enough money to take care of his family, wouldn't be successful in the long term (because there was a part of him that was just plain shy, and shyness is typically the fear of criticism), and as a father didn't want to make the same mistakes his parents had made with him; he was also convinced that his wife was secretly critical of him, but had just had never said anything about it to him. This belief, in turn, negatively influenced their relationship.

When anyone would give Bob a compliment, he would say to himself, "If you only knew how *not* perfect I am!" and "I am such a loser" or "I can't send the letters out to follow up on my leads." In reality, Bob knew what he had to do to make his business a success. He had a great service, but he had become increasingly frozen and fearful that clients or inquiries would reject him. Bob was, in fact, rejecting himself before anyone else had the chance. He couldn't handle any kind of rejection and, even if the proposal simply wasn't a fit, he took it personally, which reinforced his belief in the lie that he wasn't good enough.

Only Lessons to Learn

Bob felt better as we began to work together; in fact, he felt better from the start, as just having someone to talk to and to help him get his negative self-talk off his chest was a relief. He knew I wasn't there to judge him and that he was his own worst critic. Do you know anyone like that? I helped him to see what was possible and worked with him to shift and release the old patterns that had been holding him back. The Beaudry Process is certainly a process and not magic, yet with each visit Bob was making noticeable headway toward the person he wanted to become.

Bob became aware, during our very first interview, that the many beliefs he had held about himself had come from his early childhood. He was amazed to unearth how he had unknowingly mimicked some of his parents' unhealthy patterns. He respected and loved his parents. His father had been successful as an entrepreneur and had expected perfection out of his children, and Bob especially, even when Bob was an adult and became a father himself. See, Bob's father was also never satisfied.

In his parents' attempt "to do the right thing" by pushing Bob to be the best (i.e., "You know you are better than that,") they had also made him feel like he couldn't and shouldn't make mistakes. The more they unknowingly reinforced this message, the harder he would try to be perfect, not understanding that he was just a child and couldn't possibly know what his parents knew.

When I asked Bob to ask me if I made mistakes, he was momentarily thrown off. After he did ask me, I answered, "I never make mistakes; I only have lessons to learn." We both laughed. He considered my reply deeply and it helped to change the lens through which he viewed his life. He started to tell the truth in a way he never had before and to do his best while becoming a more effective and confident human being.

Like his parents, Bob had come to unconsciously expect himself to always be perfect, and when he wasn't, it only reinforced those early patterns, programming, and blocks that made him think he was not or might not be good enough, which were in fact lies or myths about what was possible for Bob. Some myths, of course, turned out to be of use and others were absolutely detrimental. Bob is brilliant but still felt he wasn't good enough, which only further diminished his energy and creativity, his confidence and his ability to take calculated risks. I reminded him that he, in reality, couldn't be perfect and could only do the best he could do.

Through the interview process, he started to understand that one or both of his parents also had some of the same personality traits, patterns, that were unconscious stumbling blocks for himself, as they had been for them. He then realized that he had treated his own children the same way, and he started to experience guilt. You see, Bob, like his parents, always had good intentions. He thought he was doing the right thing by his children in also pushing them to be perfect.

As we continued to work together, he began to realize that it didn't matter what he had unconsciously learned—he could learn something else. I can't help people who are unwilling to learn and evolve, but Bob was motivated to stop the pain and find relief by taking back his life as a result of rewiring his brain. I taught him that he could get out of the rut he was in and onto a unique path of success, happiness, and inner peace. Through the work he did himself (I gave him regular homework assignments to reinforce growing those new neural pathways in his brain) along with the support and overall process that I provided, Bob came to know and live as the Full Potential Highest Self he'd never even dreamed of being.

Your Conscious Mind Is Agreeing with Those Unconscious Blocks

Bob remembered that he'd hated the way his father criticized him and had treated him as a child. His father's treatment of him was a block he had struggled with his entire life without really knowing how to change it. Bob had vowed that he would never be critical of his own children when he had them. Yet he grew up to do the same thing to himself, to his family, and to his staff that his father had done to him . . . be critical!

After he became more aware, Bob realized that even though his intentions were good, he still caused a number of very good people to quit his company after he'd invested a great deal of money and time in them. He just hadn't been able to stop himself, and he secretly blamed them. He couldn't see himself clearly at that point—he couldn't be objective. This, of course, is one of the great benefits of having a strategic advisor or an emotional mentor, whether in sports, business, or life.

Bob is a good man. His emotional intelligence just wasn't in good shape. He had unconsciously forgotten to remember that he didn't want to be like his father had been. We learn what we are exposed to and grow up to express that perspective and behavior automatically . . . unless we do something about it.

He had consciously agreed at some level with his father's beliefs and patterns. He had no other early role models. He kept unconsciously reinforcing his dysfunctional patterns and blocks, thereby consciously agreeing with them. Bob, like all of us, was a master at justification and rationalization and had both unconsciously and consciously argued for his limitations because he assumed his underlying intentions were good.

As we moved to the next level of our work together, I created a guided meditation recording for him to practice with, to help him learn to calm down and relax, release old unhelpful patterns, and instill new nurturing, empowering messages.

I then taught him how his brain works and he became much more conscious and aware of his thinking, thoughts, and behaviors. Bob came to understand that he could make new decisions and enjoy new responses that matched a reality that would work well for him and for those around him. He, in fact, learned how to influence himself more effectively and appropriately.

Bob was very accomplished at his profession and had overcome many challenges in life, yet he had been living with the lifelong fear that he would fail. Roughly midway through our work together, he confided in me that even though he was a relatively young man, he had felt for years that he was going to have a heart attack before his kids were out of high school.

As Bob learned about and came to understand how humans learn and that mostly who we are is unconsciously programmed into us by the age of six, the majority by the age of three—before our conscious mind is even functional—he became more compassionate with himself. Before that he'd been an internal emotional abuser of himself.

It's also interesting to find out that more than 99% of what we know we learned unconsciously. Therefore, environment is key, but, again, we're not stuck with the past when we get the care we need.

He began to take back conscious control, and wow! What a difference from just this piece of the process. Bob would go on to raise his children in a more supportive way, while still giving them boundaries and helping them become increasingly responsible. Fortunately, he is healthy and fulfillment is no longer a dream: it is his reality.

Internal Blocks Are Not as Solid as They Seem

By learning about how the mind works and how to work it better, Bob came to understand that the unconscious mindset that had held him back and made him a worrier could be released. This new knowledge helped him understand that his old struggle with confidence was tied to someone else's perspective that was unknowingly unsupportive. Bob also came to realize they had been lies that he'd told himself because he was unconsciously mirroring the blocks and patterns of his environment. He began to realize that he had made some very important decisions from a child's perspective that we then revisited to help his "inner child" mature into his wise adult self, set him free to grow up and re-parent himself. From this part of the process, he was able to experience a self-acceptance he had never known before, as well as newfound confidence.

We worked on the aspects of his dysfunctional emotional belief system and corrected them at the whole-brain level, getting down to the core causes and correcting his self-talk from limitation to freedom. This led Bob to be open to clear the deck for the forthcoming on accessing and integrating his Full Potential Highest Self.

He's now a healthier, happier, confident go-getter—complete with a new plan for expanding his business in a joyous way! Together we brainstormed new strategies for expansion. Bob learned improved communication skills and more effective team-building strategies for greater success. He is working his plan and accomplishing what he knows works, making sure to test the waters to see what will yield the best results! And boy, it continues to pay off!

Bob no longer has those old fears. He moves forward with increased creativity and absolute confidence . . . and he's proven to himself on a consistent basis that he can take charge and be the business owner, husband, father, and leader of his company, and contribute widely in his community.

Fulfillment is no longer a dream; it is his reality. He's a happy, far more successful human being!

CHAPTER SEVEN

It's All About You, Relationship with Yourself

Shortly after Alan's retirement, boredom set in. He had looked forward to more golf and more time with his grandchildren. However, he quickly found that no amount of golf or grandkids was as satisfying or as exciting as being in charge, a rock star, so to speak, as the CEO of a Fortune 100 company.

He was a stately, regal-looking man in his late sixties. As he struggled with what to do with his life, he'd volunteered to lead a planning and fundraising drive to save a major historical site. This noble cause was a huge success, but didn't make him happy, even though he received great praise for the work he had spearheaded. In retrospect, anger lurked within him.

Alan had become very introspective over the years and, at the same time, grew increasingly frustrated at his own inability to master himself. In addition, he became conscious that he was increasingly impatient and could, on occasion, intimidate others who simultaneously admired and resented him. This went for colleagues and also for his family members. Alan wasn't a happy man.

What Is Your Relationship with Yourself?

Consider the following: Before you have a relationship with others, you have one with yourself. It was, at first, shocking to me to find out that we're already learning starting at the third month in utero and our brain is being wired even by the environment outside our mother's womb.

Experiment: I invite you to take a moment to experience what this might be like. Put your hands over your ears . . . What do you hear? If someone is talking, music is playing, the news is on . . . you can most likely hear it. The sounds or words may be muffled, but you can probably still hear them. A baby in the womb may not understand the meaning of the words, but the tone of the voice resonates and is already influencing the neurons in its brain and body; wiring him or her for the world they'll be born into.

As you remember that who you are begins in the womb relative to the world around you, in looking back on your childhood, what was your world like?

Some people say they can't remember their childhood, but you've also probably never been asked about the people who raised you and about their personality traits.

In Alan's case, he showed up frustrated and increasingly aware that he was critical of others, as well as of himself, and aware that his impatience was coming though in his tone of voice, internally and externally. There was anger underneath it all. He had exhausted himself trying to make everyone and everything around him fit within his idea of perfection.

Together we discovered he was a perfectionist, insecure, controlling, unhappy, angry at himself and blameful of others, depressed for most of his life, and emotionally disconnected from others.

He later reported that his mindset was even affecting his health. He felt tired and upset, though he put on a very controlled face (as the corporate type is most often masterful at achieving). Underneath it all, though, he felt vulnerable.

How You Communicate with Others Can Make You Friends or Enemies

As we dove into his history and self-talk, it was revealed that he had become a rather introspective man over the last decade of his life, and he was finally able to admit to himself that he wasn't perfect. Of course, this made him even more determined to get "it" right. In his efforts, he had visited counselors and a few others, had read tons of self-help books, and finally had been referred to me.

It was clear that he had been raised by very strict parents, who had modeled that he had to be perfect. Even though his parents never said so directly to him, he'd clearly gotten the message as he recognized that he was punished when he wasn't perfect in their eyes. Even though he hated this and knew it wasn't fair, he ended up raising his children with the same punitive hand. As a result, they had become distant and unreachable. This frustrated him because in his retirement he had the time to spend with them and to get to know them, but his attempts fell on deaf ears and hearts.

Alan had a quick smile and could be very charming. He admitted he'd become a master at subtle manipulation within the several organizations he had led, and had, on his way up the ladder, felt justified. He was now recognizing that he had been a bit of a "justified bully"; you know, the old "for your own good" perspective. He thought he was the smartest person in the room, but eventually came to realize that he had unknowingly been a very poor listener. He also came to discover that he was passive-aggressive—and this realization did not add to his happiness!

When asked about his friends, he simply said that his relationships with others had been shallow and that he didn't have anyone he could be himself with. He was a master at charm, yet had never let anyone get close. He had no longtime friends he could count on. To keep up his facade, he just couldn't let himself be vulnerable.

Everyone is vulnerable in some or in numerous ways . . . It's unavoidable!

In fact, as we worked together, Alan came to realize that he didn't know who he was or who he wanted to be now. He did remember setting high standards and being willing to "play the game" of making it up the corporate ladder for financial, status, and power gains. Each day was like a new ball game in which his job was to win. Satisfaction wasn't even part of the equation for him. Alan came to recognize that it had always been "all about him" to the world around him. Yet he had a loneliness within himself. He didn't trust anyone yet felt relief at even just the opportunity to share his story and discover undiscovered aspects of himself.

What Is Your Self-Talk Like?

Deep down, Alan suffered, and unconsciously he was fearful that he might not be good enough. He was downright mean to himself. Like most individuals, he was terribly hard on himself. Psychotherapy, counseling, medications, coaching, and meditation hadn't worked for him—none changed the way he felt inside. He unhappily became angrier and more frustrated, stressed, critical, and depressed, at first with others, then with himself. His self-talk had become increasingly derogatory over the years.

Working with me, he came to see that his experiences in life starting from early childhood and continuing on until the present day had everything to do with his perceptions and beliefs, how he thought and talked to himself, and how he felt inside. He was his own worst enemy. He had become like his father in that he wouldn't admit that he felt bad; he just saw himself as depressed. *Ouch!* That's a terribly lonely place to be.

So many people tell me they are depressed or have anxiety—that they've been told their biochemistry is out of whack. They may have been given medication, but hate the side effects. The idea of being dependent on medication to fix the problem isn't usually a happy one for these leaders. And, the deeper inner fears are still lurking. This is one of the main reasons people find their way to see me.

Here's the Scoop on the Majority of Depression and Anxiety

Most people who are depressed are perfectionists. Perfectionism creates a life of dissatisfaction—since nothing is ever perfect, over time that turns into anxiety or frustration. When anxiety or frustration persists long enough, many people become exhausted and eventually become depressed. It's a cycle that can be broken when they get the help they need.

How Often Do You Attend to How You Communicate with Yourself?

Many of my clients, when I first ask them about their self-talk, look puzzled, so here are a few questions for you to answer for yourself. I invite you to take a few minutes to answer these honestly. You don't have to share your findings with anyone. Just write them out and put them in a safe place. Awareness is the beginning of transformation and evolution.

More questions for you:
- What are your various (good/bad/ugly) perceptions or beliefs about yourself?
- What are your perceptions or beliefs about others?
- What is your self-talk like?
- What is the tone of voice of your self-talk?
- Do you ever feel "less than" when you try to be perfect?
- Do you get into the "shoulda, woulda, coulda?"
- How many perfect people have you ever really met?
- What standards do you hold yourself and others to that may be unreasonable?
- How do you scare yourself?
- What do you fear?

- What if you discovered that your authentic self was more than good enough and that you could simply thrive?

Benefits Alan experienced include finding inner peace, happiness, taking control of himself, and coming to appreciate the differences in others. His listening greatly improved, and he discovered his Full Potential Highest Self. The ability to settle down within and at the same time create a life of adventure and fulfillment for himself and for the woman who after forty often difficult years he once again considered his "bride," as well as for his family members was ignited.

At our last meeting, he shared with me that, for the first time, he felt at one with his life and connected to his spirituality. Thanks to The Beaudry Process, he admitted, "I wish I would have met you when I was a young man.

During our work together, Alan learned that he had new options and used them for his greater good, instead of spending all his time criticizing the people and circumstances around him. His retirement had a refreshing new meaning that allowed him to feel good about himself and his future!

CHAPTER EIGHT

Correcting Your Past, Giving Yourself Permission to Be the Catalyst

In Walt's case, he came to see me to get over a pattern he'd fallen into since the first grade. Initially he didn't know why he had this fear of public speaking because he had recently been hired as a college president at a very prestigious university in the Southeast.

He had grown up in a small town and his family was poor. He'd always had insecurity issues and felt shame that resulted in him being very shy. Shyness is the fear of criticism. It was time for Walt to learn how to become the voice of the university he was so proud to represent and to become the catalyst in his own life that he was meant to be.

Walt and I had a telephone meeting some weeks before his arrival. When he walked into my office, at first he seemed to express ease and grace. In fact, I was a bit surprised given his tone of voice over the telephone. His friendly and well-spoken tone seemed to be natural for him—nothing like the panic I had heard during our original phone conversation. Surprisingly, he explained how nervous he was to be with me in person. I assured him that I was not there to judge him, but to help him. He didn't look outwardly nervous, but he was fearful and upset on the inside. He had become a master at avoidance of his biggest fear: public speaking.

Walt had worked hard to make his way up the chain to reach his goal of becoming the college president of a prestigious university. Having been in the education system all his working life, he had always been deeply and completely committed to making a positive difference for students. It was a calling for him. He felt he had the potential to make an even bigger difference in such a position at the university.

He had been officially hired several months prior and had unfortunately been getting increasingly anxious about his lack of confidence in front of a microphone ever since. So much for his dream come true! He told me he wanted to run away every time he thought about having to give a speech . . . and he knew he'd be asking for money at many of these events. It was that fight-or-flight response we've all heard about.

Although this position was exciting for him, it was also extremely difficult because a big part of the job was to raise the school to a new level of prestige and financial security. Walt knew he would be judged at every step, and he wanted badly to leave a legacy he could be proud of. Politics, as you well know, isn't just for business or Washington, DC. Academic politics, and how a university relates to the community, is a delicate situation and a big deal.

As we continued to strategize, Walt shared with me not only his fear of public speaking but eventually his issues centering around money, the fear of making mistakes, and the overriding fear of failure.

His eighth-grade teacher had taken an interest in him and it was then and there that he'd decided to make teaching his lifetime career. He had enjoyed teaching a great deal and it was no threat to him because he knew his subject and had worked hard to be a professor who inspired his students.

I wanted to know how he felt when he experienced this fear. He reported that his heart raced, he could barely catch his breath, and he often felt faint and sometimes sick to his stomach. He'd tried everything he could to be "normal" and in control, but the harder he tried, the worse he felt. Taking medication before giving a speech had been his only recourse, but he didn't like it and knew it wasn't "fixing the problem." In fact, Walt had anticipatory anxiety that he would feel months ahead of a scheduled presentation. He could in one word describe it as "dreadful."

He went on to tell me that just thinking about having to give a speech would make him feel these same feelings and how he'd immediately begin to feel like a fraud, somehow incompetent, and judged by those around him. This was all tied to his childhood, as his résumé certainly hadn't reflected any of these issues.

A large part of his job was going to be frequently speaking to alumni, various organizations, businesses in the community, and individuals who could potentially throw their financial and other valued support behind the university. Universities are just like any other money-making entity, but he'd never really addressed his public speaking fear prior to accepting his new position. Sure, he'd gone through Toastmasters and some therapy, but his fear was so deeply rooted that he needed something else. But what?

Over the years, Walt had been pretty good at deflecting his speaking challenges by being humble and suggesting that others take the spotlight. This strategy just wasn't going to work any longer.

He needed help fast, and permanently, but had nowhere to turn, since his new job was starting in less than thirty days. I told him I was confident I could help him—with his help. We shifted his internal gears, through the use of effective interviewing and the Method's processes, in addition to strategic guidance, he began to truly evolve into the person he needed and wanted to be . . . to feel comfortable and competent to get the job done!

When we started to work together, he realized that he'd had this problem starting at the age of five, and in the years since, it had only gotten worse. I explained that how we express ourselves emotionally when we're young will tend to become more pronounced as we grow older. He found this to be true for himself. Walt acknowledged that he'd been raised by unsophisticated and uneducated people who thought college was out of the question, since it never came up in conversation in the household. His family had actually criticized him for wanting to go to college. I could relate. I had grown up in a similar environment. We had a lot in common, as I often find with many of my clients.

I went on to enlighten him about the nature of anxiety and how anxiety always comes from perfectionism. I asked him, "How many perfect people have you met?" He answered, "None." Yet, the standards he held himself to could never be maintained because he, like every one of us, was bound to make mistakes as part of learning. At first, he wanted to argue with me, much like he would argue and become critical of himself. He had been ruminating about mistakes he'd made throughout the years and was living in the past or in fear of the future.

He had decided he had to be perfect to make it and to be the great influencer he'd set out to be. As a human being and now a leader, Walt realized he could be very judgmental toward others, especially if he perceived that their behavior could potentially reflect on him. This defensiveness didn't serve him as a leader either.

Deep down he was so tense that he agreed he had no idea what being relaxed was. All that internal stress was a setup for feeling overwhelmed and fearful. When we're very stressed, we have about 1,700 different physiological changes that occur in our body and our brain. We can't always think as clearly as we'd like to or in a way that would be most beneficial.

As we continued to work together, Walt began to calm down, as he recognized that feeling calm is a prerequisite for changing the brain and the body's reactions, as well as to help retrain the brain and grow new neural pathways. As he calmed down, Walt could take in new possibilities.

Next we started to help him release the various old patterns we'd uncovered during the initial interview. He became open to truthful thought patterns that freed him up to become the leader he wanted and needed to be. Taking Walt through The Beaudry Process allowed him to calm down and think more clearly. He came to understand that these patterns were learned and that he could learn new ways of thinking and behaving. As he became calmer and more in control, he was able to easily work to release the fears that had held him back for too long. He learned to trust himself.

He is an excellent speaker because as we worked to repurpose his ability to communicate well and has fun doing it now. He was able to step up and be the leader he'd hoped he could be—especially when he experienced his Full Potential Highest Self. All fear was gone!

CHAPTER NINE

Coming to America

John's thick British accent seemed to be the beginning of what would turn him from Mr. Confident and Competent into a man of insecurities. As a COO of a large international manufacturing company, John came from the UK with plenty of experience. However, when he interacted with his American division in Georgia, he was stunned to discover the massive difference between the cultures and, often, the values. He'd been involved in teleconferences between the two offices at the top level for a number of years, but turning around operations down South was proving to be a challenge for both him and the locals. He described it as feeling like he'd moved to a different planet.

John had come to the US with not only a unique accent but some pretty strict values that didn't seem to align with the Georgia folks he was here to lead. He had no one he could confide in and no one to help him with the transition—until he showed up in my office. We went to work right away with helping him to understand and value his history, and then embrace a new culture by bringing out the curious and nonjudgmental side that he needed to reflect as the leader he was expected to be—and that was within him to be.

We discussed business, manufacturing, and leadership strategies. We talked about the latest research and books I'd read that could be helpful in integrating him into the American style of leadership: moving from being "the boss" to being the supporter he needed to become to engage the American team.

The Method helped him to challenge and embrace change. As he calmed down and opened up, we worked to build his confidence in leading within a new culture by helping him to understand the differences and ways to share his values that would bring the company the increased bottom line they were looking for. After all, this was why his company moved him and his wife to the US!

Ultimately, he regained great confidence. John evolved his leadership skills, regained his confidence, and furthered his emotional and social intelligence. He came to appreciate the differences among his staff and found our time together to be a growth and maturation process for everyone—him *and* his support—but one he will forever be grateful for! All done with the utmost confidence, of course.

CHAPTER TEN

How You Treat Yourself Is How the World Treats You

Immediately upon meeting William at my office, I could tell that he was distressed. Expecting at least an outwardly confident man, I found him to express himself as worn-down and feeling and acting like he was a loser. I suggested he stop looking for a new position until we had worked together to set him right again.

William had been at the top of his game for most of his corporate life—that is until the organization he had been leading was bought out by a new group of investors. After working for one of the largest corporations in his field in the Southeast for over twenty years, he was excited to be at the helm of the new group. He had always been confident and performed almost wizardly with the prior organization. However, the new owners were pushing him to change the way his successful company was doing business and the new style wasn't a fit for William.

He tried and tried. The new board of directors thought he was doing well, but it became very stressful for William because their ideas became roadblocks to his prior strategies—the ones he knew had worked so well. You see, William was a people person who understood the critical importance of creating and nurturing relationships over the long term. The new company was more automated and wanted everyone to cold call and use the telephone as their primary means of communication; William wanted to use to face-to-face relationships.

Finally, the day came when he thought it was time for him to move on. They offered him more money to stay, but no amount would be enough to make him want to come to work and be unhappy every day.

William expected that he would take a much-needed break that included a bit of travel and sport fishing off the coast of Mexico. After about six months, though, he decided that life wasn't as exciting as it had been when he was at the helm of a multi-billion-dollar business. He was bored.

He reached out and when he wasn't immediately snapped up by another organization, he became despondent and eventually depressed. His emotions had nothing to do with concerns such as finances, as he had done very well over the years, had invested wisely, and was, according to him, "set for life." He and his wife enjoyed their friends, travel, and a beautiful nest.

He was looking to oversee an organization that provided the level of service and satisfaction that had made the difference for his prior company and that he had prided himself in providing over his career.

Because of his state of mind and lack of confidence before we worked together, he was unemployable. Unfortunately, how we feel gets expressed outwardly without us even knowing it.

During our work together, I helped William remember that he only needed one good company, the right match, to connect with. We challenged his fears supportively, and pretty soon he began to remember his fearlessness and tell himself the truth again. As he shifted how he had been treating himself, he became the powerful and attractive leader he had known himself to be.

In the end, William landed his ideal job and both William and the company he now serves consider themselves extremely lucky. It's as if it was supposed to happen—and it did!

CHAPTER ELEVEN

Your Conscious Mind

Let me bring clarification to a longstanding myth: that the left part of the brain is logical, and the right is creative. Modern science has completely debunked this perspective. Turns out that we use all of our brain! However, our "conscious" mind is located in the frontal lobe, the area of your forehead. And the "subconscious" mind is all the rest of the brain (both left and right).

We all come with a body and a brain, but we didn't get an instruction booklet. In the next few chapters, you're going to get an overview of how your mind works in relation to your body and how your conscious and subconscious interact for your greater success—or struggles—depending on your prior environment and the messages you live with.

The following is a list of major functions in the conscious mind and how it works:

Conscious
10%
Master—adult like
Logical
Analytical
Decision maker—free will
Math
Language
Words—communication
Thinking
Creativity

Our conscious mind doesn't really kick in and start working for us until around age three or four. If you have children or have been around children, you probably are quite aware that it's virtually impossible to reason with a two-year-old, right? A two-year-old's conscious, logical, analytical mind isn't developed at that point. Volume-wise, the conscious mind is only 10% of the brain. Its job is to be the master, the leader, and the boss because it has the listed adult like (executive functioning) qualities.

In our conscious mind, we communicate with the use of words. When we're being logical, analytical, making decisions, doing math, or speaking language, we're using words. Words are very important for two reasons: not only are they the language of the conscious mind, or how we express our consciousness, but our subconscious hears all those words. Because our subconscious is hearing them, we are unconsciously programming or "hypnotizing" ourselves all the time with our language or how we take in and interpret the world around us.

A word about thinking. Most people are walking around thinking that they're thinking more than they're thinking. In other words, we are not thinking as much as we think we're thinking! Most of the time, we're actually reacting instead of thinking. Now, at least in the English language, we use the word "thinking" very loosely. Thinking only occurs in the conscious mind, and we are only present in our conscious mind for 20%–50% of our waking day. Let us explore more about this part of the mind.

Your Mind Is a Tool You Can Choose to Use Any Way You Wish

Whose mind is it? Your mind, of course. Yet, without truly understanding your mind and how it works, you are at a disadvantage when it comes to making the best use of your most powerful resource.

All Behavior Comes from Thought (Subconscious Programming or Patterns) and Sometimes Thinking

Thinking only occurs in the conscious part of our mind. For example, would one of your hands ever float over, all by itself, and take a pen from the table?

Of course not! Yet, we are typically unaware that we had a thought about it before we proceeded to do it.

Let take a moment to distinguish between thinking and thoughts. You've learned about the conscious mind where thinking occurs. Now a word about your subconscious: Thoughts, on the other hand, are all the programs, patterns, and "automatic pilot reactions" from our subconscious mind. Humans have about 70,000 thoughts on average a day, some more and some less, of course. Now you know why you can't just quiet that mind of yours! However, you can improve the quality and effectiveness of those thoughts by evolving your inner perspective.

Thinking Is Required

Do you know how to use a computer? Would you ever have learned how to use a computer without using your thinking mind? No, of course not.

You had to think (use your conscious mind) about the computer and focus to learn how to work it for what you wanted it to do for you. Over time, you likely created a sequence in your head and then walked yourself through that sequence and constantly rechecked yourself, right? Repetition is the mother of learning. And because you did that, not only did you learn how to use the computer to your benefit, but you shortened your learning curve and many projects you use the computer for are practically mindless in terms of how to use the computer.

Any time we use our thinking mind, our subconscious mind is on high alert, which helps us learn and retain information faster, shortening the learning curve. The good news about a computer learning experience is that it gives you instant feedback. You don't have to guess if what you're doing is working or not. Human's aren't that cooperative and most of the time we think of the feedback as criticism.

Thinking is required to change any behavior or learn something new. And repetition is the mother of learning. Yes, sometimes we learn something forever, such as a traumatic event from a one past experience, but otherwise true automatic response learning takes practice to be unconsciously great at the new behavior.

In order to effectively change, we need to change our thought(s) and ultimately our belief, which gives us the ability to change our internal program or become open minded. This allows us to change our behavior, or *doingness,* making it is a lot easier to do.

I'm not saying that it never requires any effort, but it's a lot easier to achieve when we get our whole brain involved and focused in the same direction about something we want to learn or achieve. In other words, if you want to learn to play golf, you would naturally expose yourself to golf, learn and practice it, rather than expecting that taking tennis lessons would be helpful.

It's not enough to tell yourself to just change the way you're thinking, as you well know!

Now, let's move on to the other 90% of your mind . . . the subconscious.

CHAPTER TWELVE

Your Subconscious Mind

Subconscious
90% of your mental capacity
Childlike
Memories
Habits
Creativity
Emotions and feelings
Images and pictures
Autonomic nervous system
Reactions

Now we're talking about the other 90% of our mind.

Reviewing brain development for a moment, we communicate with words in our conscious mind and while the conscious mind kicks in and starts working at about age three or four, our subconscious mind begins to learn during the third or fourth month in the womb. So, for about six months before we're even born, we're hearing words and sounds. We do not know the meaning of those vibrations, but it doesn't mean that they're not affecting or influencing us or that we're not already being programmed for the family or culture that we are born into. Not to mention the effects of such things as the tone of voice, our mother's response or reaction to the relationships and world around her, and her physical and mental and emotional state.

Ninety percent of anything is going to have power, but in this case it's quite childlike. We're going to refer to this childlike part of the brain as our two-year-old, as an analogy for the vulnerability of our subconscious mind at any age, which will always be or potentially could be as vulnerable as a two-year-old child. This is also a potential explanation as to why we all can act immaturely or inappropriately from time to time.

A two-year-old does not know right from wrong, good from bad, a lie from the truth, imagination from reality. All a two-year-old knows is what it is getting exposed to, or ultimately what we keep saying to ourselves throughout our life. Think about how you talk to yourself. Your self-talk may not always be to your benefit or yield a positive outcome. Or maybe it does. Most of us have some of both from time to time.

Without realizing it, you're programming yourself with every internal and external message. Very often, these programs came from the people who raised us and from society or social situations. But we take them on, even when it is not always in our best interest to do so because the subconscious doesn't know any better. That's why working with someone to help you become more conscious and intentional is important.

How often do you come up with a negative thought and you don't even bother to argue with yourself? In fact, it's likely that you unconsciously just agree with it.

You don't think about it; you're not logical and analytical about it. You're reactionary. You react to the program in your mind and you then wonder why your life doesn't change. Remember that all behavior comes from thought. If you don't change your thought, your behavior is not likely to change. So think of it as if you have a two-year-old inside your brain.

If you had a two-year-old, you wouldn't expect them to know what to do to evolve and become a mature adult. It takes a commitment from parents and others to potty-train that child, for instance. And it isn't something that you'd just say one time. You, as the adult to the child, would make the decision for the child when it was time. Following up on that decision, you would become observant, consistent, and support the child to be successful (for everyone's sake). And you would optimally give praise rather than be critical or punitive. How many times would you do this? However many times it took, and it would typically be many times, depending on the child. Ultimately, it finally happens when the child decides to be "grown up" and do it themselves, when they get the connection between that sensation in their body and take on the personal responsibility to manage it themselves.

So think of your subconscious mind as something that needs to be retrained. You know how critical you are about a particular pattern within yourself? Has self-criticism made your issue go away? No. It probably made it worse. So the key is to give up criticism, decide what you want, and begin to take yourself to that new place in your mind. See yourself doing your new choice, behaving that way, acting that way, regardless of how it's been in the past. It takes paying attention. It takes self-correction. And often it requires support. Remember, telling yourself to "just change the way you're thinking or behaving" is easier said than done.

A couple more things about your two-year-old. You can never send this child inside your head to the babysitter. This child is with you 24/7 and thinks you know what you're talking about, even when you say things to yourself that aren't in your best interest.

It's important that you know the research is clear that environment makes THE major difference in the personality and behavioral development of all human beings.

Think of it this way, because I want you to be careful with how you talk to yourself. If you have a thought or pattern that comes up three times, it's already a hardwired program. Listen to those programs that are already going on in your brain and begin to self-correct. If you're having trouble mastering your mind, The Beaudry Process can teach and support you. You can get there with effective support way faster than on your own!

I have one more comment about the two-year-old. Your subconscious mind could really use a responsible adult (your conscious mind) to help influence and correct it.

Everyone knows that we have a nervous system, but most people don't realize that it has different components that do different things. For instance, the brain and the spinal cord are called the central nervous system. We have other components, but we're concerning ourselves here with the autonomic nervous system. Literally every thought you have is communicated throughout the body. That's why when you think positive thoughts, you tend to feel pretty good; you think negative thoughts, you feel badly. Our nervous system is an electrical system so the transmission is very fast!

Do you ever experience stress? We're the ones who are actually creating stress for ourselves. We say that stress is out there, but the things out there are really stressors or potential stressors. We're the ones who, by the way we think about and deal with life, decide whether a thing is stressful or not. You know how some of your colleagues are stressed out and some of them aren't dealing with the same issue? It all depends on how you are thinking about something, how your own mind is wired—your perception of it.

The autonomic nervous system is what was once called our involuntary bodily reflexes. We're only aware of 4%–5% of the energy around us. Physicists have determined that everything, all matter, is energy vibrating at different frequencies. Have you ever had a moment when you walked into a room and suddenly felt horrible? You felt tired, drained, upset, or any number of other emotions. Or maybe you've noticed that when you're around a particular person, your mood changes, for better or worse. That's energy, pure and simple. We are made up of energy. Everything around us is energy. Our thoughts? Those are energy, too. Think back to the experience above: walking into a room and suddenly feeling heavy; you don't want to be there. There are negative vibes in the room. It works both ways. If the thoughts or moods of others can affect you so profoundly, it's not hard to imagine how your own thoughts affect you and your environment!

Take a moment to think about a negative pattern or emotion you struggle with. Now, take a moment to look back at the list at the beginning of this chapter that relates to the subconscious. Your problem has been a memory. It's become a habit. Certainly, it's not the most creative way you could choose to live—you don't want it, you don't like it, and yet it persists even though it's not in your best interest. You've rationalized and justified it. And still, it hasn't gone away.

Why? Because that's not the answer. We're creative beings; that creativity allows us to come up with new options. But, it's easier to remain unconscious and stay stuck in the rut. We often don't even see a way out without feedback and support.

Remember the proverbial two-year-old in your head? If a two-year-old wants to do something that could hurt him or her and you scold them, they're not necessarily going to stop. They're going to most likely want to keep at it. But if you show that two-year-old something else to focus on that's positive and safe in a joy-filled tone of voice, they'll tend to stop and move on to the new option. As with a child, it may take some reinforcement for yourself, but it can be done.

Now, focusing again on the subconscious list above, let's think about it with regard to an issue you may have. Although your negative pattern is not a creative option, you can give yourself new options (remember it's like a two-year-old). It's definitely tied to your emotions and feelings, as well as to images and pictures in your mind's eye. It's a reaction; it's affecting your body, your thoughts. That entire pattern is a reaction.

Reactions are mostly unconscious. We don't know what to do about them. We spend 50%–80% of our waking day in the subconscious alpha state. That can sound kind of scary, but it is a good thing we have our subconscious mind. Although in this example we're focusing on a negative pattern, we have tons of great programming in there that helps us all the time too! For instance, you don't want to have to learn how to drive a car every time you get behind the wheel and you have great resources within you that you access daily without having to think about it.

Everything depends on your perception—the programming in your brain. If something in the subconscious isn't working for you, you can use your conscious mind to help reprogram it. However, it's important to recognize that the subconscious is also known as the unconscious. Our subconscious knows way more about us than our conscious mind ever will. So to correct old repeating patterns, it's critical to access the subconscious to correct them, which is not something you can really do for yourself. If you realize that you're unable to master an aspect of your programming and are tired of suffering, remember, successful people ask for help when they need it.

As mentioned earlier, words are the language of the conscious mind. The language of the subconscious mind is expressed in emotions, feelings, images, and pictures.

I tell my clients, "I don't have problems—I have challenges and opportunities."

I also tell them I don't make mistakes. "I haven't made a mistake in years, but I still have a lot of lessons to learn."

By reframing how you talk about things to yourself, you can and will change how you feel inside. Changing the perception changes your reaction, moving your thoughts and processes toward being solution-oriented and creative. The subconscious mind is much like a movie, a series of pictures. What generates those pictures in the subconscious mind are the words that we use in our conscious and that come from our subconscious programming.

Your subconscious mind is a massive database full of patterns and habits, right? It just sits there unless something comes along and triggers a thought or unless we intentionally choose to focus on something. Have you had a thought and lost it a split second later, not remembering it? Thoughts will come and go: if we choose to focus on one, then it stays there and keeps coming back. We use our words to enhance thoughts or decide to let them go. And another thought will show up right behind it. It's not unusual for many to experience the looping of a thought that just doesn't seem to want to go away.

But how can we intentionally change the way we perceive things? How can we give the subconscious something else to focus on? Remember, it's as vulnerable as a two-year-old and can be taught anything. I suggest that you be persistent, patient, and encouraging in your self-talk and actions.

If I tell you not to think of a pink elephant, what comes to mind? Of course, a pink elephant. To focus on what not to do or what you do not want simply will not work. That only reinforces the problem.

What does work? Redirection. We can redirect the subconscious much like we would a child and offer a new option rather than to reprimand. And, as humans, we are really good at beating ourselves up by focusing on what we want to stop doing or what we don't want. That pattern drives us further in the opposite direction than the one we deserve to move toward.

All behavior comes from thought. If you change your thought, you can and will change your behavior, sooner or later.

CHAPTER THIRTEEN

Putting the Conscious and Subconscious Together

I like to use the analogy of the mind related to business. The conscious mind is like the leader. The subconscious mind is like all the other people working for your company. You are interdependent with one another. Every company needs a leader or the company couldn't thrive or even exist. Yet without all the support from the employees, the business would likewise not exist.

The conscious and subconscious are similarly interdependent, as different as they are, and are absolutely communicating with each other. Bottom line, the words we say to our self or how we interpret the world around us is the cause of how we feel and what unconscious energetic messages we send out into the world. Most people live in the illusion that your thoughts are just in your skull. But since everything is energy, your thought gets transmitted out into your world and affects those around you. Therefore, you can imagine what it does to you. Your employees are highly influenced by your spoken and unspoken messages. What messages do you send out? Praise or criticism? Appreciation or impatience, for instance? Are you even aware?

We have our conscious and subconscious minds, but how do they connect? By communication! What difference does it make and how does it affect our ability to be to be successful, since this connection exists?

First, let me explain with yet another example. If what is holding us back is some kind of fear, the good news is that fear is a learned behavior versus an innate response such as breathing, and can be transformed into a different belief through working with the whole brain.

For instance, I have another client who was so anxious that his body would simply shut down. This worrywart pattern affected him in a number of ways. Not only was the stress at work (from running his company to hiring new management and getting them up to speed) killing him, he wasn't as healthy as he thought he was physically. In fact, during this period, he had a heart attack and was one of the lucky ones. And stress crept into his personal life and influenced his love life. Really, how sensual are you going to feel if you're worried and all stressed out? He was also a perfectionist, but this physical response and the emotional response that came with it felt to him like one and the same. They do interrelate, and to him it seemed like an innate response. Certainly, something he was unable to control, something he didn't want to happen. It's not like he had a choice.

He hadn't always had these problems. He'd gone to the doctor thinking that his sex-life issue was a remnant of his prior heart problem, but he checked out just fine. He didn't want to take pills to make his love life better, so he wondered if I could help him. He'd remembered meeting me at one of my speaking engagements and called.

He came in confused and distraught, of course. He speculated about many terrible things that could be wrong with him, including the doctor misdiagnosing the "problem."

He had anticipatory anxiety by this time. He was in a fairly new marriage and had lots of pressure coming from everywhere, but mostly from inside himself. He had no one to talk to and didn't want to go to a therapist. He just couldn't get into the idea of it taking a long time to get "fixed."

By taking him through the Method, I helped him learn to calm down. He learned about his mind and how to use it better. He came to understand the mind-body connection. We did lots of housekeeping, so to speak, to clear out lifelong patterns of negative thinking that he'd not even realized were unconsciously running him. In his case, he came to understand that he had been experiencing PTSD, too, which we also cleared.

He became increasingly masterful at how he was communicating with himself and his new team at work. With this new information, he began to feed his conscious and subconscious mind the real truth. Without realizing it, he had become masterful at scaring himself with old immature and limited perceptions, all the while trying to be more and more perfect. Being in business for years, he realized there was no such thing as sustained perfection, but deep down those old unrealistic expectations of himself that he'd been raised with kept creeping in, until we addressed and corrected them. His marriage is happier, too!

The Truth Will Set You Free

We've all heard the phrase "The truth will set you free," and the truth really will set you free. Fear is a learned behavior—if you can learn fear, you can learn something else. Think for a moment of an issue you have, a pattern or habit that you're not happy with or that is a problem for you. Go back to chapter twelve and review the subconscious list relative to your issue; give that some thought. You will start to see how your pattern or issue is a memory or a habit. The most creative way you've ever learned to live is tied to your emotions and feelings, images and pictures. This affects you physiologically and is a reaction.

An emotional reaction that the body responds to is different than something that is biologically or otherwise innate. I want to challenge you to be more aware of your thoughts and become aware of your bodily feelings that may be telling you that you are stressed out. And if you don't know how to get past it, find the help you need. Hanging on to the past does not serve you! Don't kid yourself about how you think you're objective, that you are so smart that you should be able to figure it out and get rid of the problem. You haven't done it yet, have you? You're too close to the problem and do not have the understanding of all the programs and patterns that are affecting you from your unconscious mind.

You are also encouraged to ask yourself, at any given moment, who is in charge—your conscious or subconscious? Is your adult mind or your two-year-old in charge? It's all about retraining yourself for success. It doesn't matter where you've come from or what traumas you've been through. It doesn't matter what beliefs were dumped on you by other people or what limiting thoughts you have within yourself; it doesn't matter what mistakes you've made; you can learn to lead with your conscious mind in charge, making new goals and objectives to move you forward. You can learn to use your conscious and subconscious in concert for your greatest success. Remember, it's how we generate emotions that work and don't work.

Most people are walking around thinking that their conscious thinking mind is running the show, when in actuality they tend to operate from a more subconscious, reactionary, and emotional state—even if they don't want to admit it.

Of course, when you're in business, you'll look at the numbers, the bottom line. But when it comes to making that final decision, if you're not sure which way to go, you'll start listening to your intuition. Intuition is something that's part of the makeup of your mind. It comes from experience; things either make sense or not, and you either have a good or a bad feeling about it. That's where intuition comes in, puts it all together, and then lets your gut talk first and then listen to see if it knows what it's talking about. It may encourage you to take a calculated risk when the numbers say it could be iffy. Or are you operating out of fear and stopping yourself from your greater potential? We need our whole brain, and your heart and your gut is part of that brain, too. We are hard wired and science has proven that the heart in your chest knows before your brain knows. Intuition is a conscious and subconscious body experience.

There are no guarantees in life, you know that for sure. You have to remember that it's your thoughts and beliefs that generate those feelings, and because of that you have the capacity to become enlightened, to be in a state of true choice, or to become the person that's possible for you as you evolve and awaken to the possibility of experiencing your Full Potential Highest Self, with help.

Parts of your life or your whole life can be in a rut, but it doesn't mean that you're stuck there or that that's your true path, the one you were meant to follow. It might help you to remember that as much as you want to control everything around you, it just isn't going to work. How well do you control your own self? Remember, no one is perfect.

So, as you stop lying to yourself and begin to surrender the illusion that you can control the world around you to some degree, it's important to remember, are you going to criticize yourself and others? Are you going to trust yourself and others? Experience over time builds confidence and you're the one who's helping to achieve this. Praise yourself and understand that this year you're more evolved than you were last year and last year you were more evolved than you were five years ago, so appreciate yourself. And, *breathe*!

You are the artist of the outcome of your life! All you have in life is time and how you use that time determines your outcome. Every day you're consciously and unconsciously molding the clay of yourself and influencing and affecting those around you by the choices you make, the thoughts you have, and the reactions and behaviors you exhibit. You are a powerful influence on many and more than you'll ever know. Are you committed to leaving the world a better place? You are in a position to do so by becoming healthier and a more authentically successful leader who is happier mentally, emotionally, financially, spiritually, and physically. You have every right to succeed.

What I want to leave you with is that sometimes people get caught up in the notion that they don't or might not deserve good things. That's one myth that some of us picked up along the way, but the truth is that we all deserve good things, so long as they are healthy, respectful of others and yourself, and create a win-win situation. You deserve good things—material things, wealth, joy, love, health, peace, and happiness—no matter what your history has been or the regrets or mistakes you've made. It was inevitable because making mistakes is part of learning.

By the new choices you make, you build upon the evolution of your life. I encourage you to be persistent and patient with yourself to simply and lovingly correct yourself and then move forward. You can do it and you *do* deserve it. And you can ask for help if you need it. No one experiences their Full Potential Highest Self alone. You are and can become more than you ever imagined yourself to be.

What doesn't work is that we sometimes use our emotions to harm ourselves, which turn into addictions. All addictions are an attempt to give to ourselves. So it's not the alcohol, drugs, sex, gambling, shopping, and more—it's simply because you're not feeling whole inside. Understand that there's nothing wrong with giving to yourself; you just need to find appropriate ways to do it, just like you would in business. If something isn't working in business, then you find another way of doing it . . . You don't let yourself stay in the rut of what's not working.

CHAPTER FOURTEEN

You Can Get Results Faster!

What is the benefit of knowing so much about the world around you, if you don't really know yourself? Remember, 90% of our mind is unconscious. No one can fully know oneself, yet I have worked long and hard to help leaders access and correct those stressful and unhelpful patterns that keep them from their greater good.

The interview is the beginning of relief toward greater acceptance or identity of self and others. Ah, just to get it off your chest in the safest of environments—confidentially and nonjudgmentally. Insights from this introduction to the process are often utterly amazing and a great way to begin to awaken. I've shared that we learn from our early environment, and here's some very good news: *If you learned that, you can learn something else.*

The problems may be inside you, but so are the solutions! Talk therapy or coaching alone is just touching the surface of the complex being that each of us "thinks" we are. The Beaudry Process, coupled with my caring support, can make the timely difference that most leaders are looking for.

Leaders in every field are human. Yes, you are human. It may be painful to hear. It is more painful to experience a state of denial. Perhaps you feel too human. It's okay!

Even if you do not struggle from emotional issues, you strive to improve yourself; you want to be an even better leader. That takes work and accountability. It takes someone near you who can be objective.

Leading by example and instead of fear, perfection, or being unreasonable toward others around you isn't leading in the most effective way. The old design of the "boss" as the leader simply doesn't work in the twenty-first century. You really aren't the king or queen. You may be the leader, but people choose to follow you, or not. At least in the US, we have freedom and often amazing options.

Although you may feel that you cannot show your vulnerable side, the truth is that everyone is vulnerable from time to time—no matter how smart or experienced you are. The Method helps you learn to navigate to the finish line and know that you have lived up to your Full Potential Highest Self.

We are especially vulnerable when it comes to our subconscious mind, coupled with our conscious mind; creating whole-brain learning and rewiring is an important key to helping you to control yourself instead of merely reacting to your environment or to your own limited internal perceptions. Learning to be proactive instead of reactive is the key. You know that this is optimal in business, but most people don't know how to successfully transfer that understanding to help themselves. It's often said that we can see the solution for others, but not so clearly for our own self. Again, being completely personally objective is truly impossible.

Another problem is something called cognitive dissonance (inner conflict). This pattern is common to most humans but is not helpful in leadership. For example, you are a great leader, but your company struggles or you blame your staff for not getting the job done.

You want to blame others but don't want to accept that the buck stops with you.

Perhaps you've tried coaching—even for the entire company—yet within a period of time, things are back to the same old rut with only some minor shifts because deep inner change has not occurred.

Perhaps you've tried coaching, therapy, or counseling for yourself or others—like your wife, your operations support, a board member who has an ongoing anger reaction, your struggling sales force—yet they also don't seem to permanently change. They look to you for guidance. They need you to be a great, healthy, mature leader.

Why? Because their problem or pattern lies deep within their subconscious mind. All you or others see are the outer and often unhelpful effects of this pattern.

Perhaps you are blind to your own shortcomings and no one will tell you because you will not invite them to or you will only hear it as criticism. Perhaps you don't trust anyone.

Those closest to you might be afraid that you will punish or reject them or stop loving them. If they are already feeling this way, you don't have the kind of relationship that would make them want to stay with you. You might not know how to make it safe for them to engage you or share their perspective or experience. Really, how safe are you with the way you talk to your own self?

When Jack Nicholson said, "You can't handle the truth," the reason the statement was so powerful is that on some level, we can all relate to the message. And, yet, the truth is the beginning to open yourself up to charter a freer, more effective course.

What the Method offers is relief and deep inner correction, leading to

- inner peace
- greater self-mastery
- greater awareness
- improved leadership and communication skills and outcomes for you, your company, and your family—professionally and personally
- greater profitability
- greater productivity

- happiness
- a clear mind
- increased resourcefulness
- increased creativity
- awakening and integrating your Full Potential Highest Self

What Is The Beaudry Process?

With your help, the Method will help you to correct and rewire your mind and body consciously and unconsciously to achieve the results that give you inner peace and self-mastery.

Strategies? The Process and Combination, Customized for You to Produce Benefits Resulting from

- Awareness interview: awakening to your experiences and early orientation and provides opportunities for new choices.
- Relaxation and release of patterns that no longer serve you and perhaps never did.
- Learning new skills along the way to discern new strategies and opportunities for effective communication and joyful leadership.
- Education: As individuals and groups come to me to have me help to influence

them, I always ask, "Who's the most influential with yourself?" The answer, of course, is their own self! Since we don't come with an instruction booklet, I teach each client how their conscious and subconscious mind works and how it affects their body to a much greater degree than I've had a chance to share with you in this book. I also teach them how we create and change habits and patterns. This gives them some very powerful tools to become more aware and to possess skills that are truly doable to develop and promote greater personal transformation on a daily basis.

- Why Cognitive Conscious Mindfulness? Regular talk therapy, counseling, or coaching can never, or at least rarely, get down to the unconscious root causes of habits and patterns that are at the core of our struggles and poor decisions. This customized-for-you strategy allows you to create new updated and mature choices that will give you the results you crave and deserve!
- Ongoing assessments: In order to make sure that you are on track and stay on track for greater evolution and creating effective patterns, it's important to check in at each meeting.

- Focused goals: Make strides each time we meet and reach desired goals over time. Create new options, new coping skills, improved communication skills (both internally and externally), as well as changed behaviors.
- No matter what you learned in the past, if you are capable of learning, you can learn a better, healthier, and more effective leadership style of thinking and behaving to model what you are capable of and to influence the world around you more successfully for all . . . including you!

Put the Method into action and you get faster and more permanent results than anything out there, based on research, feedback, and practice over the last forty years!

You can set yourself free to become even greater than you are now.

You can meet and integrate your own Full Potential Highest Self to live the life you've dreamed of. You are the key! Together we can help you become the leader that those around you need and want.

You Have Special Gifts and Talents

In case you don't recall, you came into this world with all the gifts and talents unique to you and that can be shared with others. Remember how each person is recognized as being perfect at birth? You were too! When did you become imperfect? Maybe you never did but didn't get the memo. Maybe you were inundated with negative, fearful, perfectionist feedback . . . maybe meant to be in your best interest. Or maybe you think your parents were perfect and that you have no underlying issues that constrain what is possible for your future. If that is the case, that would be highly unusual and unlikely because no one is perfect. And, if you are a narcissist, it truly is "all about you." If that is the case, as perfect as you may think you are, most narcissists are really very insecure inside and resist change. They are less likely to ever really be a team player and have issues perhaps beyond my capabilities to help.

Many people, deep down inside, are afraid they may not be good enough or that something is wrong with them. I know I felt like that at one time. If you're one of the many, you are good at scaring yourself. And you've also probably become good at hiding it . . . yet it plagues you.

On the other hand, if you think you are too good, that's also a problem because it holds you back from valuable resources that could support you in being the leader you deserve to be. When I ask people, "Do you like liars?" They invariably tell me, "No!" I then ask them if they ever considered that they may be lying to themselves. At first, they seem confused because they think that whatever goes through their mind is pretty much the truth and factual. Hint: You really can't believe everything you think and say.

Your subconscious mind is too filled with beliefs and perceptions that may be tainted to fit what *feels* comfortable or familiar but is still unhelpful.

Would you like to stop lying to yourself? Is it time you saw, experienced, and learned to tell the truth about yourself and life in a healthier, more prosperous, and happier way?

The Beaudry Process uncovers the real truth about each human being—that you are whole, perfect, and complete in your own unique way! Would you like to start respecting yourself and creating a life where you feel whole, perfect, and complete in your own unique way? A life of learning, without criticism? A life of joy and freedom to evolve into the person that is possible for you to be and that you feel great about being? The person you perhaps never thought you could be?

I invite you to seriously ask yourself . . . Take a moment and make note right now, "How am I stuck in some uncomfortable, unhelpful, or unhealthy pattern in my life?" (PAUSE and breathe.) Transformation begins with being honest and open in a safe environment.

This is a process . . . not one magical pill . . . not one step and you're done! As a strategic advisor and emotional mentor, I help leaders with individual leadership and team performance.

The one thing you can do to start the process is to get clear on what it is you really want. And to begin to be willing to change the way you think about your role and what you're doing.

What If You Don't Do Something about Those Blocks Holding You Back?

Well, you and those around you will continue to suffer and experience stunted growth. This is not the path to anyone's higher potential.

What If You Do Something?

You can have what my many clients have found, but in ways that work for you in order for you to awaken your Full Potential Highest Self, to feel at home and peaceful within, and to be successful like you've never experienced before!

Imagine for a moment
- being thought of as a truly great leader
- leading a top company where people find satisfaction in working as a team
- writing and publishing that book you've always wanted to write even if you don't know how
- leaving a legacy that you could have never left had you not awakened to your Full Potential Highest Self

What's Next?

I challenge you: Pick one thing in your life that you believe is holding you back from experiencing your Full Potential Highest Self? Then ask yourself if you want to change that pattern. It starts with you making a decision that you want to improve your life, your leadership, your world.

Know this: You are unlimited potential. You really can be smarter than you have been in the past. You can learn to get out of your own way to experience wholeness and joy and still make a ton of money!

You are part of the most powerful force in the universe. You are a unique and magnificent being with special gifts and talents. You deserve to awaken and live as your Full Potential Highest Self. It's the creator's gift to you. Embrace it today!

> "Consultants for me weren't the answer, as I know more about my company than they'll ever know. Someone introduced me to Jane Beaudry. She quickly assessed my situation, helped me clarify my blind spots, and moved me toward a new level of being competitive in the current market."—Richard K.

> "You are very good at what you do. Your insightful and thoughtful approach helped me understand what was going on in me and

where my behaviors originated. Your extensive background was obvious. Your insights into the people of influence in my life and their motivations and leading me through understanding them were invaluable. I liked your quiet and unemotional approach to helping me. My only regret is that I did not find you sooner. Thanks for a happier, more successful, and more satisfying life."—Alan P.

You are invited to take your own free self-assessment to begin to become more clear for yourself.

BusinessRelationshipsAssessment.com

After the 2 minutes it takes to complete this, you'll receive feedback immediately to learn more about you.

ABOUT THE AUTHOR

Jane Beaudry
President
MasterExecutiveExcellence.com
jane@MasterExecExcel.com
(404) 276-8789

Jane's honed and famous therapy skills have been sought by executive leaders from all over the world for over three decades due to her deep level of commitment to getting right to the point, as quickly as possible, to get relief from destructive patterns that prohibit a full and expansive life. Jane boasts a full toolbox of skills and methodologies to shorten the long and tedious process that others work with to get desired results. Many clients confidentially call upon Jane in a neutral position stating that they are happy, but not fulfilled or just want to improve. It is only in working through their patterns that they unlock joy and love for life and a passion for their endeavors. After working with Jane, clients report that their business flourishes, their personal relationships are real and meaningful and that the inner peace with themselves that they have discovered is priceless.

Jane is a strategic advisor, best-selling author, keynote and breakout speaker, businesswoman, executive coach, and wife. Jane currently resides in Atlanta, Georgia. Her practice comprises clients that see her in person, by phone, and with video technology.

www.ingramcontent.com/pod-product-compliance
Lightning Source LLC
Chambersburg PA
CBHW070257230526
45470CB00002B/624